W9-AYC-056

Parts That Were Once Whole

~

Margaret,
Thanks for your

Parts That Were Once Whole

support & good leadership.

Poems by Nancy Botkin

Nancy

~

MAYAPPLE PRESS   2007

Copyright © 2007 by Nancy Botkin

Published by   Mayapple Press
               408 N. Lincoln Street
               Bay City, MI 48708
               www.mayapplepress.com

ISBN   0-932412-49-1
ISBN+13   978-0932412-492

Acknowledgements:

Poems in these pages have appeared in: *The Flying Island,
Poetry, Maize, The Midwest Quarterly, No Exit, Passages North,
Poetry East, South Dakota Review,* and *Sycamore Review.* "Poem
with Light and Dark" won First Place in the 2005 Maize
Poetry Prize Competition sponsored by the Writers' Center of
Indiana. "Letter to the Water Dept." and "Signs of LIfe" were
included in *Who Are The Rich And Where Do They Live?*, an
anthology of contemporary American poetry published by
Poetry East. "Geometry" was selected by Ted Kooser for his
national newspaper column, *American Life in Poetry.*

This book would not have been possible withouth the gener-
ous support and encouragement of my family and friends.
My sincere thanks for readership and other forms of essential
support go to: Jacquee Dickey, Mike Amato, Phyllis Moore-
Whitesell, Tom Vander Ven, Ken Smith, Joe Chaney, Stephen
Meats, and Richard Jones. Deepest thanks to David Dodd Lee
whose critical insights and suggestions were invaluable; and to
Judith Kerman for her faith in the book, and editorial direc-
tion.

Cover design and book design by Judith Kerman with titles in
Lucida Sans and text in ITC Giovanni.

Cover art, "Left Out in the Rain" by Jacqueline Dickey, from
the private collection of Mike Amato.

What do you feel in your mouth
scarlet and thirsting?

—Federico García Lorca,
"Ballad of the Little Square"

~

for Dave and Kelsey

Contents

Three

And So It Is

It's everyone's story—yours,
mine, the Mexican singers
gathered around our table
in Nogales

with their accordions
with their guitars and maracas
and their deep, sweet voices.
A tragic song about a girl—
bonita—a lullaby.

Two fingers of which hand touched
the lips of another in a grove,
woods, back yard, Buick?

What songs do we sing and to whom?

The body's truth
located in the pinwheel's whirr
isn't clear until it slows, until
each bright point stutters.

The lion stretches on the savanna, licks
its crimson muzzle.

It's about singing in that kind of temple.

One

~

You Again

I'm in that half-state between
   sleep and seeing your hands
   in the dishwater, your
   cellophane face on the windowpane.

We're light years apart now.

But
   I've rubbed my heart
   on the same dry star. So,
   firmament of memory,
   what more now?

How else can I burn?

Lights, Memory, Action

1.

I have to steady myself when memory
starts to rock,
when the world becomes a constant noise:
a ticking, a hammering,
a corruption,
a place to begin.
In its purity the world pulsates,
and like a strobe light it astonishes
with its absences.

2.

Back in the day when my father
had something to prove, when anything
he never had as a kid was a speechless
blue jewel, my mother ironed
his white shirts, creased his slacks,
listened to his dream of moving (east side
to west side), and slowly gave herself
over to cigarettes, her own private island.
The brief flare of the match dressed
her face in lemon spark,
in sparrow song.
My own pace quickened
Go to
Go to
I pulled encyclopedias off the shelf,
studied constellations, gazelles,
those wonders that sketched a map
farther out, knowledge a jutting river,
a pulsing blue vein.
Beyond the screen door I saw her pitch
the match into the butt pot,
a perfect hit, but
there was nothing she could do with that luck,
nothing.

3.

By then desire had set up shop,
and we were transfixed
by colored lights, marquees,
buying and selling.
The parade went on and on
down the stately boulevards, past
street lamps, elms, television sets
and toward the blinking antennas
where death is weightless,
where memory is fiction.
Moonlight pressing the window,
kisses darkening her flesh.
Someone peers through a keyhole.
Who's rocking in that breathless light?

4.

Pulled down by gravity, the pearls
fall to the hardwood floor.
Slowly at first,
and then in a rush
like rain.
Bouncing pearls. Luminous.
She sits in a chair
clutching her neck. He falls
to his knees.
They could be made of stone.
They could be the white, weathered
statue in the town square.

5.

The rhythm of life begins in childhood
and includes doors that whiff and then click
shut, silverware that scrapes, bed sheets
that snap, maps that unfold,
and again and again the single match
drawn across the book.
It's the rustle of trees, potatoes

dropped into oil, stairs that creak.
It's the world's traffic—
the big talkers,
the sad shoes, the angry waves
and steady wingbeats.
What does one do
with one's confusion about loving
the smell of sulfur?

6.

Finally it all comes to rest
like the ball in a roulette wheel.
The priest says the necessary prayers against
a backdrop of flickering candles,
and we turn our hungry faces to the light.
In the pew in front of me
a father loses patience with his restless child.
"Who taught her to climb on furniture?" he spits
at his wife.
After Mass, a neighbor runs after my mother to tell her
she is going to have another baby. My mother
offers her so little back. The future begins to assemble:
the baby wrapped and handed to her.
It has no choice but to latch
onto her breast and follow her into the world.

7.

However you begin, it's about the self,
finding a way to be through the passage of time,
through its twisted, troubled streets.
You try to locate the action,
the meaning, and hold it like a coin,
feel its hard surface, its ridges.
It's fumbling in the dark for shape, for form.
It's about recognizing *the lack of*,
and in the right light you can see it,
it can take you there.

Inheritance

I have my father's silver pens.
I have a gold apple on a gold chain.

But what they gave me is a body,
and she will turn against me.
I take care of her because she has a daughter.
I move her forward, the only direction
she can go. Every night I lay her down,
and every morning I raise her up.

What concerns me is how well I tell the story.
What concerns me more than ever
is that what I make is a kind of song.

Who are you?

Where did you get that?

It shines.

Another Passenger

Some remember my mother's pearls, a palace of white
igniting her wrist, or her throaty laughter,
a different kind of jewel.

I remember the white slip of her skin, how
she mourned the rain as she lit cigarettes, ran
her fingers through her hair, how
she rode a slow train as it took on passengers.

My God, wasn't it, after all, blood,
phlegm, a pebble in the windpipe?
When you enter memory, you disturb
the delicate face of the world.

On what bed, in which space, in whose field can I love?
The tiger inside the cage rolls out his pink tongue
and stares back at me
with a beautiful indifference.

I look down at my body as if I can't believe it's there.
I can't stop traveling into the ashes that float above this
city.

Don't speak
unless you want to make my ears blind,
my eyes deaf.

Parts That Were Once Whole

If you want to absolve yourself of all sin
say goodbye to your father
by measuring a rum-thin drug into a small
plastic cup and looking into his blue
eyes as he tells the story again of youth, his dream
to open a car wash in a Detroit neighborhood.

Walk down to the pond on a summer morning
and sit on a stone amidst the dragonflies' blue
worrying and acknowledge that you're just a visitor.
There are two worlds—this one,
and the one you want back,
and you ride shotgun in both.

How many times have you been under the spell
of a goodbye, say, when a plane rushes over the runway
and sunlight splashes your aging hand,
your wingless shoulder, and soon everything
with a shape and a color fades away.
Or in church when prayers that are meant
to be more than a wave to the dead
hover over the wooden pews like winter birds
with cold and fragile bones.

Go to Rome or Greece if you like to see ruins,
parts that were once whole, and feel
the absence, which is a lovely thing,
as is descending the twisted and chipped
steps of your battered self.

Expect all walls to crumble.
Live the most holy way: expect the plaza
to empty itself of tourists and tradesmen
and its ancient yellow light.

Doors Closing

I'm not there in the hotel room where a book on the dresser
is opened to a page I've read a hundred times.
Words assemble and reassemble
while at the museum I have turned my back
to the paintings on the wall, preferring to take
their images to a place in my mind
where they flicker like candles
or shuffle along like monks with their heads bowed.

An automated voice says *doors closing,*
doors closing, and the subway car glides
forward like an animal, with only a future.

The way you have to endure the world
is to go through its tunnel where, say, you're assigned
a desk at which you pray, at which you run
your finger over the gold cross in your hymnal,
at which you drink your milk from a thermos.
And then, with only memory to guide you,
you ascend its escalator, slip out
onto its window ledge to look at the faces,
the platforms, the billboards. If you're lucky,
you make all the stops.

If you were here I'd whisper this in your ear—
you can see your own image in the flat black marble,
in its lacquered surface. It's a mirror.
It's your D.C. souvenir—
not what the blonde child said at the wall
squatting, pencil in hand, to trace her grandfather's name.

I really didn't get it that good is what she said.

So you shuffle along keeping your hands free, your ear
tuned to the click of the door, and what rushes
forward, what bursts with enormous
brilliance—wind, wildfire—
will speak or it won't
as you move deeper and deeper into your blank paper.

Oh, Father

Remember that summer's heat?
It was the summer of love, and the summer
of drownings—in lakes, in pools, in ponds.
It was the summer of the barbed wire fence.
You threatened to kill a man and sped off
with your anger and your tools
after seeing your daughter's mangled ear.
It was rubble and ravine, wrench
and revolt, and the sweet lake of fire.

I'd like to say that the yellow roses, the ones
that were a gift, died slowly,
the way I like them to die—the petals curling,
their edges singed.
I've never known what to make of the joy I feel
when flowers come apart.
I love the sighing wind that pulls
bougainvillea petals across a blue pool.

I'd like to tell you, Father, about the Mexican
man asleep in his chair in the shade,
whose brown hands were locked together
like a beautiful question, lost in a dream
of a great sea flashing, doors of sapphire, of silver.

And what do you do with cruelty and beauty—
those bodies of water
that will stop you cold with their perfect
reflection of clouds and stars?

We can wake with such a hunger, don't you think,
for anything the world has to offer?
What would we do if nothing called us?

Back in your city, I peer into the abandoned nest.
The speckled quail eggs are primitive.
Motionless.
Sunlight, Father, bathes everything in this kingdom.

This Lifetime

Last night I dreamed of my youth.
When I woke in my body, it ached
with history, the roundness of the past.
A dream in which my parents were whole
as I once knew them. I woke heavy,
something missing,
something I can't get back.

It is evening and the heavy scent of peonies
floats across the room—a prelude
to a fall.
I touch my tongue to their magenta petals
just to see.
They taste of the red and blue in Botticelli.

This poet searches for a word, kneels,
waits to receive it like a holy visitation,
a word without end,
a world unreachable,
like those high windows they used to open
with a long stick, a hook.

I exit a restaurant in which the waiter
has served sea bass, has dribbled
red wine on his impeccable white apron.
There's a crescent moon and near it bright Venus
unlocking the night,
unlocking memory,
unlocking the frail, distant cities.
Venus who shines for nothing and no one,
not even the stars waiting behind the curtain,
no singing to usher them in.

Whisper *mother* into night's forever
and it blooms like a flower. Say *father*
in that same church.

There's the fullness of a door,

a door made of wood.
It's pink and worn, and there's a broom
leaning against it.

It's beautiful in this lifetime,
it's beautiful in the next.

The Lost Serenade

What is there to say about winter?

There's always blood on the snow, but whose?
Man, beast? Who walks with purposeful gait
from house to shed to field
swinging scythe or ax?

Hands slide into fur-lined gloves.
White tissues blot red lipstick.

Tongues loosened by coffee and cabernet.

My mother's landscape like her own mother's:
lost between this country
and another, this life
and another.
Each at the kitchen window marking day's end,
each at the counter separating cloves of garlic,
each at the stove stirring the sauce.

This odor of childhood survives.
And the distance it plunges through.

They weigh almost nothing.

From Dust and Ashes

The tongue says *sweet*, so you give it berries.
The mind says *sweet*, but

all you can give it is the story of your life,
which is a story of the masses.
You can give it history
and then a dream of history.

You want to dream, but not of slaughter,
not of spilled blood
which comes like a refrain, or sometimes
like a rest in music,
and silence splinters
the self.

You'll go anywhere in the world that will take you
from dust and ashes,
but what you have is a travel guide to Rome.
Start with ancient churches.
Start with San Clemente with its fascinating layers.
Start with frescoes and twisted columns and mosaics,
a different kind of destruction,
sweet, really,
something the mind wants.

Use a torch
          appreciate the beautiful
fresco

head of a bearded man.

Navigate the cobbled streets, finish
with goats' cheese, radicchio.

You look down at your body
and there she is, and whether it's a dream
or not, you give her credit for trying
to be beautiful.

The truth is
the fracturing of the world is the oldest story.

The blood's been spilled.

You've been dreaming of the world, and you want to tell
someone.

Without Ceasing

Begin yourself in the muscular dawn, gold
Splash of loneliness making its appointed rounds. . .

Unlock the arms, disentangle the legs,
Let go of *we* and feel the *I* surging,

Screaming, though you're the only one
Who can hear it. You and everyone else.

You'll be back later with your heart, bright
Flask, to swing in the moon's easy hammock.

Two

~

Skates

In childhood you unfold the map
of the world and smooth it out
with your small hand, and with one finger trace
a path somewhere not very far, usually
a block or two from home where the pond
is frozen over, where the trees sag
a little from the weight of ice, where the birds
are talking their language of pearl
and pit, where the creek
has stopped its constant complaining.
You arrive there with your new skates,
you try a little spin, and you spend
the rest of your life with that image.
Not the branches or the brambles,
not the pale moon,
not even the birds,
but the skates, all white and amazing,
there below you
at the end of your body.

Geometry

All the roofs sloped at the same angle.
The distance between the houses was the same.
There were so many feet from each front door
to the curb. My father mowed the lawn
straight up and down and then diagonally.
And then he lined up beer bottles on the kitchen table.

We knew them only in summer when the air
passed through the screens. The neighbor girls
talked to us across the great divide: attic window
to attic window. We started with our names.
Our whispers wobbled along a tightrope,
and below was the rest of our lives.

Cow

Some days a question will arise
like a cow in a field and walk over
to the fence and stare at you
for a long time with big sad eyes
until one of you looks away.
And when you return home,
you tie up the newspaper with string,
wave to the neighbor, reach
for your robe and slippers.
And the cow continues to graze,
brightens a little in the moonlight.
In fact, is nourished by stars.

What It Takes

It's not easy to get the mind to own nothing,
to let it come to rest like a swing
in a playground because it takes all
your concentration to stare
at a spot on the floor and ignore
the wind that lifts the newspaper just slightly
off the table, or the bee
that bumps the pane of glass,
or what gold key unlocks whose dark heart.

Or it's erasure, a flight,
a slipping out of the dress of the self
into the privacy of the mind
where fantasy abounds—reverie, gorgeous
and glossy, and you have to have reverence
for the mind that says you are not who you are,
but a fragment, a stormy activity, clouds
of blown dust like the immaculate stars
that don't care what we do with our lives.

What We Do

The mind is silver, a lump
of gleaming pins. Hard
to follow any one pin to its end.

That's the rush—
word and then word and then word.

A wheel burns inside the chest.
That's the heart breaking through.

A diving board above an empty pool
is a tongue. And below
is the mouth, rough cavern.

In one corner a dust devil whips
dirt and dry leaves.
That's the voice rising up.

The seasons are electric. Sweet,
sweet juices wiped
with the back of a hand.

A body can be parted like a curtain,
and a red scar closes the wound.

That's the human going forth.

Toward an Understanding

(1)

The truth about the world
is that you do everything to hold
yourself in it.
Even though there is so much blood

to clean out of the grout.
Even though you're careful to bring
the dark green liquid just up to the line.

Sky as shelter, you start loving the quilt
of clouds. You start loving architecture,
the stone pillars and the steel beams.

This is a story about denial.
The daughters want to fly out to visit
the father, but the father says it's too soon
because to invite them is to admit
that death is near.

The father holds on to the daughters for balance.
They walk him around in a circle
from kitchen to living room.
He takes small, deliberate steps forward.
They compliment, he scolds.

They try distraction.
They drive around and focus on landscape:
cactus, mountain, blue.

The doctor finally calls back.
From the other room you hear the voice
fray, you hear that it's threadbare.

Let's say you do everything not to break.

Let's say you can't pour the medicine
into the shot glass fast enough.

This is a story, finally, about endurance.

(2)

After a day of shuffling, after
his dinner is too late, too cold,

she tucks him neatly into his bed,
the fresh linens he asked for. His arms

are folded across his chest outside
the covers, his face gray, his lips white.

Between breaths he says, "Tomorrow
will be better." And then my sister leans

over his body and kisses his forehead.
Amazing, as it was when we used to play

games together. Shut inside the closet,
we stood side by side and looked down

at the light made from the squeezing down
and the shutting off. Below us a clean white

line, and we would run our finger
under the door as if through a flame.

(3)

I don't need birds to tell me I'm in another world.
All day the quail scurry by the glass door
in their impossible hats.

I don't need the desert landscape—purple cacti,
sky the color of an Ohio Blue Tip.

Just the two of us in this rocky boat, you
extending your hand to accept the glass
of dark medicine, wind tearing the words

from my mouth. You nodding your head,
handing over the map and the oars.

(4)

The slow edging into sleep.

In the dream I take his hand
and lead him to the piano.
I try to play Bach, but my fingers
stick to the keys.
He's looking away, rubbing
his hands, picking lint from his jacket.
And then I'm no longer me

but a marble statue
and we're not in the old living room

but on a golf course
and he takes out his carpenter's tool
his level

and kneels on the green

ignoring my pleas, my stormy wings,
all the cracks in my face.

(5)

And what of waking from the dream?

Not yet
sunlight on the sill.

Remember the crow trapped
in the garage? How it pulled
a string across the cars?
Somewhere
there was a nest.
Somewhere
there was a home.
Not yet.

(6)

We ride the thorns—
sorry I'm   such   an   asshole.

And in the dresser mirror behind us
evening blooms, pungent and dangerous.

Contains the larger field of wild flowers, the smear
of pollen, stroking hands, a scattering of plumage,
the preening blackbirds, open mouths, stitched
up wounds, the crawl of witchgrass, the crackling moon—

a world uncurling—

some flecks of red,
water to the lifted head,
the innocent cloth.
The inculpable cold cloth.

(7)

This is a story about beginning.
It's time to go now.
I'll take the pens and the pictures,
you take the watch and the ring.

We must leave this relentless sun
that reveals everything.

That glint in the sand was a pocket knife.
I thought it was a coin.

I walk back into a world where the blade
of everything gleams, into a world
where there can be no rest,
where there is so much joy in that light.

Friday Afternoon, Turning

I don't know where I started—me,
the self. So I'll just point
to the small schoolyard overlooking the highway,
or further inside the brick building to the room
with the nicked benches and the tall teacher
and the swinging door,
to the pristine white plaster animals
I slathered with paint and shellac,
to the paper snowflakes,

to the lanyard chain
on which I hung a whistle,
to the padded dirt where I flopped
and leapt and had the terrible fight
on the teeter-totter.
Me cracking with fear,
going up and up . . .

So I end up here, for now,
with my books and my blunders,
my files, my faith,
and my grudge, me
making myself, turning
in the heat, burning
in the body of the world.
How lucky I am to live,
to have been born.

The History of Ourselves

Why suddenly in winter
when birds fly out of the cage
of a tree, does the history of ourselves

flutter up, its dark freight
startling us, like the clear
toll of the church bell, or the train's

whistle sounding in the distance,
those quieter intrusions
when we raise our head just slightly

as the story of us floods
the bones, and it could be
anyone's afternoon

anyplace,
anyone's weak February light.

Fantasy

When you're young,
the world is small.
You have an attic room,
a bed, a rosary in a wooden box.
You have a bottle of toilet water.

You have a sister
who sleeps with her mouth open
and a brother who throws rocks on caps.

You have a creek nearby that endlessly
gurgles, dragging stick and bone.

The world pleases you,
but you want more.
You turn to your books
and this enlarges your life.

So what you end up with
is a real life and an imaginary life.

It's easy to confuse the two.

You twirl your umbrella
as you walk to school.
The leaves rain down from elm

and ash, the morning air is tinged
with smoke, and there's a delicious
melancholy you hope will linger.

It's so sweet it almost crushes you.

I Hand the Flowers to My Teacher

The lilies of the valley grow
close to the house where
it's mostly shade. There I am,
home for lunch, with a fistful
for my teacher. Not too far from me
is my mother who kneels and stabs
at the dirt with a gloved hand.
My father's shirts hang upside down
and flail in the wind.

I hand the flowers to my teacher,
and she puts them in a paper cup.
After the honeyed note flows out
of the pitch pipe, most of the voices
rush over it or under it.
One or two marry that note's purity,
its clarity. One or two nest inside
the bowed heads of the lilies,
in the hushed space of the lily-bells.

Engaged To Be Married

After we protested, the cigarette's
orange glow was like a primitive
campfire keeping danger at bay.

The smell of sulfur filled the parked car.
"If I'm going to die anyway,
what's the difference?"

And then she cracked
the window and tossed the match.

The awkward silence became a truce.

Explain to him my mother
before the cancer. Did I conjure

them, the two seed pearls she added
to my necklace when I was sixteen?

Grief

She was silent but alert during our last visit,
after the plane touched down and I landed
at the foot of her bed, stood in a room so neat
and ordered, and she sat up in bed, her head
nearly bald, a few patches of hair like soft feathers,
her hands clasped on her lap, proper and silent. It
was March and it was trying very hard to be spring
and my mother was trying very hard to say
something to me, she was trying hard to push
herself up from under the frozen layers that had
covered her for such a long time, but it was too
much, too late now that her body was so given over
to death. So I looked at her and grief looked back
at me and all the grieving that had ever been done
seemed to stare at me from two small wild eyes,
like those of a bird, newly-hatched, its beak
opening to the air, to whatever will give it
the strength it needs to enter the world of flight.

The Earth, Dark Now

I have just said goodbye,
and I place my feet on the earth
smudged with grays and washed-out
greens and browns, the dull
colors of early spring.

I go forward where yellow sticks
poke through a thin layer of snow
in a field transformed by snow and fading
light and gusts of wind.

The red sun is dropping, snarled
by bare branches, a maze of questions.

A lone figure walks the curve in the road.
Will he go to the white house ahead,
or somewhere beyond it, over the hill?
I wonder if someone will be waiting.
Whether there will be food.

And everything looks like it must go.
The colors, the walking man, and, eventually,
the moon into the sky's invisible seam.

The earth is darker.
The good people are turning on their lights
or lighting candles so that those of us
who must feel our way
can find our way back.

Funeral

It didn't seem right that it should be May
or that it should be so blue. It didn't seem
proper that birds should sing or that the air
should be so still or that someone should think
to buy a loaf of bread or pick up the laundry.
I thought these things as we stood there, our
shoes sinking into the dirt. It didn't seem
right that the Kentucky Derby should run later
that afternoon when we went back to the house
where people drank and drew numbers. Nothing
seemed right, but I didn't say anything. I kept
quiet about the sun and the blue air, about birds
and jockeys' whips, about flying manes and smooth
strides across the finish line. I said nothing about the
wreath of roses on the tired, glistening winner.

Silence

There's a prayer in it, sameness.

It's there in the steel fence, in the
hundreds of diamond shapes looped

together like lock-stepped Vegas dancers.

And in the paint cans stacked in a pyramid
on the showroom floor, and in the lines of trucks

angle-parked on the lot, windshields gleaming.

Where something ends another begins,
sometimes as far as the eye can see.

But what prayer
among the men who emerge from the cornfields,
white robes, hoods,
marching together in unholy pattern?

What silence
so evident in the stalks
growing tall together, rain-washed?

What secrecy
there in the twisting silks,
husks aflame?

Drought

Early on the heart recoils,
learns to mistrust. How much
is too much?

With one foot pressed against the truck fender,
the farmer tugs the bill on his red cap
while the TV newswoman interviews him.
The rain he's been waiting for has arrived.
But the downside—

and we hold our breath.
The big afternoon sky all around him.
New fertilizer needs to be applied.

The rain washes it all away.
The cost.

Or—
the photo of the woman taken
just after her winning number is announced.
More than shock
or disbelief.
Wide-eyed and both hands
shielding the heart.

And the lover—
after so many failed loves—
caught off guard in an unexpected turn
toward the sun. A fortune.
Even if it ends tomorrow, I really haven't lost...

The heart here flushed
and curling inward
like the child moments before
the birthday party who can't come out
from under the bed
or the blanket to face the abundance.

The Heart Ripening

Take the brokenhearted one
on a drive down a long country road.

Show him the Midwest,
the utter expanse of it.
Glide by the corn in neat rows.

Turn onto another road, straight
and squared off.
Right as rain.

Tell him he can sing, you do it
all the time, no one will hear him.

Wave to the stranger
driving the opposite way.

Point out the lush field,
the sky so blue
a man could weep.

Trust him when he leans out the window.

Trust that the wind
knows how to touch a body.

Love Poem

What could be more simple
than a sky with nothing in it?

Or a few white petals stuck to the bricks?

But it's more than that.
Those of us who have stood
in the field, walked the path know.

That man with his head in his hands
could be trying to remember the order
of presidents, or he could be thinking
that the world is too much—
the sky, the broken bicycle wheel
spinning in the wind.

The only choice is to love the world.

The trees are almost bare,
and the leaves rush in one direction
and then another.

Lazy Eye

My heart opens and closes on a rusty hinge. . .

Attic room: our dolls with their slim legs and bubble
hairdos lie on the floor like so much human wreckage.
We shut ourselves in the closet
with our glow-in-the-dark rosary and touch
the whorls in the wood paneling—black
eyes, ghosts, open mouths signaling gloom or glory.

I fumble inside memory, smudge its fingerprint.

I project myself into the wallpaper
in the doctor's office. I am that fancy
lady with the bright parasol and trailing
ribbons standing next to the horse and buggy.
I follow that image around the room.

Someone shouts me out of that dream—
my mother, or the nurse all in white
who tips my head back and drops
the colorless liquid into my eyes,
my lazy eye.
I try not to confuse the details:

the stiff cap,
the dim room, the soft
clicks, the shrieking sunlight,
my spangled and star-lit youth.

Signs of Life

The man on the radio says other intelligent life is quite probable, given the size of the universe. Imagine the other life in their cars, leaning in to listen through the static, slush falling from their boots. And when their stony-faced moon, full and bright, casts its evening glow, do they stand beneath it, look to their hands where that light is reflected and make some promise, a resolution, maybe, that will carry them to spring?

Three

~

Poem with Light and Dark

I keep silent vigil, my heart held out,
a beggar with a cracked rib, an oily
wrist, as Sister in her spotless wimple
delivers the facts in a cold boxcar.

We roll toward 1965, and all the great
calamities are behind us or have yet to occur,
and my good eye, the fierce one, the one
that tracks truth or the gardening crew

outside the rectangular windows is singing
in a different key, crooning in the season
of gills and sleeves and messengers
who deliver the good news from balconies.

A wind, light as a secret, ruffles the papers
on the top of the radiator
when the girl with the gap in her teeth
falls into epileptic seizure. First the slap

of the desk, and then she's a barking seal.
Sister tries to control her flailing arms, orders
all of us to face forward. A few are grateful
for the interruption, but we'll confess that sin

later under the guise of another sin, behind
a closed curtain, our hand making its ritual cross,
heaven forgetting for a moment its radiance.
"Where you have light you have dark," a painter

once said, not a famous one, but a man on TV
as he dabbed titanium white on the tip
of his mountain. When the sun turns the great
machinery of afternoon, the trees begin to climb

out of their misery, and a scrap of paper
makes an appearance, flattens itself against
the brick briefly
before leaping, before flying.

Bone Vision

For days I watched my father eat
less and less
until he stared at his food
as if it were alien.

And then that vision!
Those dark, musty roadside huts
where they sold animal skulls—cow,
mule, buffalo. Hundreds hung on the walls.

The curves were beautiful—
perfect, really, ghosts of the desert,
stark and silent.
Two hollows where the eyes
used to be.

And the hawk overhead—

Do you suppose from that distance
the body's hunger could be seen
as a sacred thing?

Personal

Again when you turn around
something clarifies itself,
a long hunger subsides. Anger

sits quietly near the fence.
What you want to do is look
at the teenagers' fingers entwined.

A tattoo on her inner arm,
his breath in her mouth.
They wear the face of all that is possible.

The almost invisible light from the stars
looks in on you with so much clarity,
their distant emergencies explode

and you gladly bear their weight.
Those yellow roses on the table
like released breath

or like a child at the pool gulping air.
They arrive in their splendor,
casual-like, but brimming with death.

At the fountain you see the teenagers and water
gushing down the marble steps. They've slipped
their coins into afternoon's vest pocket.

Soon the sun is waving all its banners,
smoke rises from the wick, and you find
every fallen petal in the cup of your hand.

Tuscany

In the dream there is a train
and a track stitching up the field.
And in the field, red poppies.

A woman sits alone in the dining
car wearing a jacket, a hat.
The light has the quality of a past

century. There is a secret
behind her vacant stare.
She slowly pulls the gloves

off her hands. The rain
has so much patience,
a lullaby on the poppies.

Letter to the Water Dept.

Dear Sir: Our water is bad. We live in the city
and when I fill a glass and hold it to the light,
I can see the debris. It's cloudy and flecks
of different color and size are floating everywhere.
What is this? Sand? Nitrates? In the morning
when I turn the water on, for a few seconds the smell
is rotten. Are the pipes shot? Do we need a filter?
My hairdresser lives in the country and her water
comes from a well. She told me she has iron stains
and that her water softener is not doing the job.
My neighbor's basement is crumbling. He's down on his
knees examining the cracks and the peeling paint.
There's seepage, he says, and the walls are moving.
The paneling in our family room is warped. We take books
off the shelves and they're covered with mold. The children
wake me, they want cups of water in the middle
of the night. They drink lemonade too and like to chew
the ice. My husband bought a dehumidifier and empties
out gallons of water into the laundry tub. He tells me
not to worry, but sometimes I feel the floor buckling
under me. Trust me, he says, and then he reaches for me
and his hands are light and moist like dew, or like the misty
rain that hangs in the early morning fog.

Door

Nothing delicate about it.
He said *shut the door* and then
turn around.
But she looked anyway
when he took a trowel off the shelf
and dug into the seat of his pants
with his spastic hand.
One crutch fell to the garage floor
and then the other.
He leaned into the wall
and then brought it out
shit
his own shit
and then his mother at the door
telling her to go home.
All the way she saw the bikes,
ropes, swings, and bats
of the children who had not yet
crossed over into the world.

Unearthing

for Linda

Morning changed her. The silence
and the weak light. What was usually
made of stone, floated. The dew
on the grass gave her the courage to weep.
Darkness, too. She stood under the moon's
bright light as faith, as prayer.

And rain.
She heard the taps and smiled.
When it fell like needles, she began to say please
and wait. After the deluge, she began to ask
why and how much and for whom?
Now there is scent, sweet scent.
She can offer the fruit from the bowl of her heart.

Trains

Everything gets out of the way of a train
says my husband on the drive to the station,
and didn't I dream that I didn't (get out of the way),
or was it a bus headed for Canada, somewhere far,
out of this country, and didn't the woman
sitting next to me offer me pennies
from her wallet, counted out four or five,
maybe they were almonds, brown and sweet,
a gesture, a kindness, but not enough for the fare,
and didn't the driver shout and order me off
as everyone stared at me in disgrace, the kind
I suffered at the hands of my father
as he tried to build his life quickly
and correctly, by himself, all that intricate scaffolding,
without a blueprint, and now these thoughts
come roaring through and the questions are awful,
how to get from here to there, how much
to ask for, and from whom.

White Wedding

Ribbons of light, the light
of late summer fell
on the patio, on the white
tablecloths that covered round tables,
on the white plates.

We were young.
We didn't have expensive dresses
to wear to the party, just cotton prints,
polka dots or flowers.

We ate our meal in stages, salad first,
not the way we were used to eating.
We tapped our gold-rimmed plates
with heavy forks and knives.
Elegance. Ecstasy.

There was a future assembling
somewhere far off
and I wanted to get there.
I could get there faster
holding a fluted champagne glass,
listening to the melancholy notes
of a string quartet.

Those same notes were making an older woman's eyes
well up. She bit her lip
and stared off into the trees.

I see now that what she was resisting, I was courting:
Let summer turn to fall.
Let all the tomorrows come.

How To Leave a Country

A woman washes her car
and I think of Picasso's *Woman Ironing*.
In the painting there is a small bowl,
not far from her hands, that is scraped clean.
This woman, like Picasso's woman,
is bent over. Her hair hangs in loose
tendrils, and she is in deep concentration.
She drags her blue pail without a handle.
She moves her torn rag in a circular motion.
Soapy water creeps down the driveway like lava.
The other cars sweep by quickly.
It's easy to see the beauty, to love
the hands that will someday perish, to leave
all the countries that death owns and return
to them with rags and soap and water.
To fill the empty bowls, to empty them.

Autumn Sky

Some nights it's simply
the size that bothers you,
and on other nights, it's predictability.
The way the stars take their places
like obedient school children—

hopeful, blinking.
But it's you
who wants to be filled
with knowledge.

And you can't stop yourself
from extending your hand,
fresh from its dark pocket,

as the moon lowers its shade
and the hopeful faces fade away

in a direction that everything is going.

Mosquito Poem

The air is alive and eggs
float in the stagnant water
in the lids of garbage cans

and in the standing pools near
the streets and in the ditches
and back by the fences

in Indiana where the rain falls
like a sermon this June in
a church where all that lives

bows to something else.
One clings to the opposite side
of the screen door, its voice a sacred

hum, blood held in the chalice
of the belly from which eggs tumble
and larvae spill so brazenly into

the ponds and the pools of water,
rising in numbers uncountable and
circling in the evening air, little halos,

holy, no beginning, no end.

Conjugal

Under a blade of sun, a sky
in which I've already drowned,
the river is calm,
one of those in-between towns
a train passes through without fanfare.
It flaps its lazy flag of desire,
it goes on.

It's easy to love the way a river holds an image.
There's beauty in reflection: black branches
crisscrossing, the arch of a bridge.
The river moans when it's disturbed,
when a duck tumbles into it.
Or is it the sky that cries out,
bruised so precisely?

Peonies

Let the clouds do their drifting

while the moon runs through its phases
exactly as it must.

Let the light stream through this kitchen
window, glorious light.

Did you ever come apart so slow

that the hands around you, fluttering,
swift hands, buoyed you, brushed

away the misshapen, burnt
edges of you, all evidence erased?

Let the heart expand and contract.

Light, irrefutable dark.

Thousand Island Lake

From the sky the eagle
watches the loon

tuck its head under water.
The people on shore watch

the eagle's graceful wheel.
Those inside watch the coffee

brew. Neighbor watches
neighbor's boat motor slowly

across the lake. They raise
their cups and pale steam rises

above their stunned hearts.
Hummingbirds flit from hemlock

to feeder, feeder to hemlock.
The new century stalls, a car

that won't turn over. It catches
just as the deer bolt after standing

still like stones—or the dead
who shake us again and again.

About the Author

Nancy Botkin was born in Detroit and spent her youth in Michigan. She received a B.A. in English from Michigan State University in 1978 and a Masters in Liberal Studies from Indiana University South Bend in 1990. Her poems have appeared in numerous journals including *Poetry, Poetry East, The Midwest Quarterly, Passages North,* and *South Dakota Review.* Her chapbook, *Signs of Life,* was published by No Exit Press in 1999.

Nancy lives in South Bend, Indiana, with her husband and teaches freshman composition and creative writing at Indiana University South Bend.

Other recent titles from Mayapple Press:

David Lunde, *Instead*, 2007
    Paper, 72 pp, $14.95 plus s&h
    ISBN+13 978-0932412-485
Zilka Joseph, *The Lands I Live In*, 2007
    Paper, 42 pp, $12.95 plus s&h
    ISBN+13 978-0932412-478
Johanny Vásquez Paz, *Poemas Callejeros/Streetwise Poems*, 2007
    Paper, 74 pp, $14.95 plus s&h
    ISBN+13 978-0932412-461
Larry Levy, *I Would Stay Forever If I Could and New Poems*, 2007
    Paper, 60 pp, $12.95 plus s&h
    ISBN 0-932412-45-9
Christine Hamm, *The Transparent Dinner*, 2006
    Paper, 90 pp, $15.95 plus s&h
    ISBN 0-932412-44-0
Kathleen Tyler, *The Secret Box*, 2006
    Paper, 74 pp, $14.95 plus s&h
    ISBN 0-932412-43-2
Rachel Eshed, *Little Promises*, 2006 (bilingual Hebrew/English)
    Paper, 104 pp, $16 plus s&h
    ISBN 0-932412-42-4
Angela Williams, *With a Cherry on Top: Stories, Poems, Recipes &
Fun Facts from Michigan Cherry Country*, 2006
    Paper, 130 pp, $17.95 plus s&h
    ISBN 0-932412-41-6
Lynn Pattison, *Light That Sounds Like Breaking*, 2006
    Paper, 98 pp, $16 plus s&h
    ISBN 0-932412-40-8
Lorraine Schein, *The Futurist's Mistress*, 2006
    Paper, 44 pp, $13 plus s&h
    ISBN 0-932412-39-4
Rhoda Stamell, *Detroit Stories*, 2006—our first fiction title!
    Paper, 102 pp, $18.50 plus s&h
    ISBN 0-932412-38-6

For a complete catalog of Mayapple Press publications, please
visit our website at *www.mayapplepress.com*
Books can be ordered direct from our website with secure on-
line payment using PayPal, or by mail (check or money order).
Or order through your local bookseller.